Fact Finders™

Land and Water

The Amazon River

by Mike Graf

Consultant:
Robert M. Hordon, Ph.D., P.H.
Department of Geography
Rutgers University
Piscataway, New Jersey

Capstone press

Mankato, Minnesota

Fact Finders is published by Capstone Press
151 Good Counsel Drive, P.O. Box 669, Mankato, Minnesota 56002
www.capstonepub.com

072010
005869R

Books published by Capstone Press are manufactured with paper
containing at least 10 percent post-consumer waste.

Library of Congress Cataloging-in-Publication Data
Graf, Mike.
  The Amazon river / by Mike Graf.
    p. cm.—(Fact finders. Land and water)
  Includes bibliographical references and index.
  Contents: The Amazon River—The Amazon's path—Exploring the Amazon—The
Amazon's people—Using the Amazon—The Amazon today.
    ISBN-13: 978-0-7368-2482-8 (hardcover)   ISBN-13: 978-0-7368-6160-1 (softcover)
    ISBN-10: 0-7368-2482-0 (hardcover)   ISBN-10: 0-7368-6160-2 (softcover)
    1. Amazon River—Juvenile literature. [1. Amazon River.] I. Title. II. Series.
F2546.G74 2004
918.1'1—dc22   2003015054

Editorial Credits

Erika L. Shores, editor; Juliette Peters, series designer; Linda Clavel, book designer and
    illustrator; Alta Schaffer, photo researcher; Eric Kudalis, product planning editor

Photo Credits

Ann & Rob Simpson, 1
Bruce Coleman Inc./Laura Riley, cover
Corbis/Royalty Free, 22; Wolfgang Kaehler, 11; Yann Arthus-Bertrand, 6–7
Houserstock/Rankin Harvey, 10, 16–17, 19, 26–27
North Wind Picture Archives, 13
Stock Montage Inc., 15
TRIP/J. Sweeney, 4–5
Victor Englebert, 18, 20–21, 23, 24–25

Artistic Effects

Image Ideas Inc.

Table of Contents

Chapter 1

The Amazon River

The river swells and overflows its banks. Dark, muddy water flows onto land where green plants and tall trees grow. Water as deep as 30 feet (9 meters) covers the land, turning it into an underwater forest.

Fish called tambaqui and arowana swim through the underwater forest. They eat insects and fruit on tree branches.

Each year, the world's second longest river floods. Animals and plants living in and around the Amazon need the yearly floods to stay alive. The high water helps fish and other river animals find food. River water also carries seeds downstream to rich soil. There, new trees and plants will grow.

Water covers areas of the rain forest each year when the Amazon floods.

The River

The Amazon River flows 4,000 miles (6,400 kilometers) east across South America. Only the Nile River in Africa is longer. The Amazon River has more water in it than any other river in the world. Almost 20 percent of the river water flowing into the oceans comes from the Amazon. People sometimes call the Amazon "the ocean river" because it is so large.

FACT!

Each day, the amount of freshwater from the Amazon River flowing into the Atlantic Ocean could provide New York City with water for 11 years.

The Amazon River is 6 miles
(10 kilometers) wide in some places.

Chapter 2

The Amazon's Path

Small streams flow together high in the Andes Mountains in Peru. The streams create the Ucayali and Marañón Rivers. These rivers rush down the eastern side of the Andes. Near the city of Nauta, Peru, the rivers join and flow into the Napo River. Together, the rivers form the Amazon.

Thousands of **tributaries** join the Amazon River on its path to the Atlantic Ocean. These rivers add water and **sediment** to the Amazon. The Negro, the Madeira, the Tapajós, and the Xingu are four important Amazon tributaries.

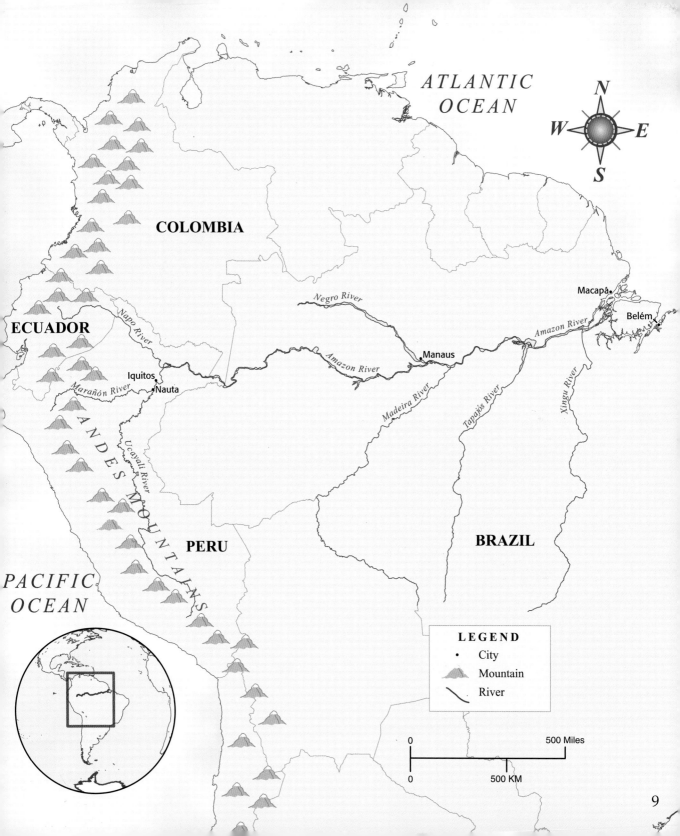

ATLANTIC
OCEAN

COLOMBIA

Macapá

Negro River

Belém

ECUADOR

Napo River

Amazon River

Manaus

Amazon River

Iquitos

Nauta

Marañón River

Madeira River

Tapajós River

Xingu River

ANDES MOUNTAINS

Ucayali River

PERU

BRAZIL

PACIFIC
OCEAN

LEGEND
• City
Mountain
River

0   500 Miles

0   500 KM

In the Rain Forest

The Amazon River flows through the world's largest tropical rain forest. Here, trees grow so close together that little sunlight reaches the ground. Rain falls daily.

The rain forest is full of life. Millions of birds live in the trees along the Amazon. Fish and insects in the river are food for the birds. Anacondas are huge snakes that feed on animals living in the Amazon River. Jaguars are wild cats that hunt for deer and other animals near the river.

Macaws live in rain forest trees along the Amazon River.

▲ Fish are sold at markets in the port city of Belém, Brazil.

Into the Ocean

The Amazon flows through **channels** as it nears the ocean. The channels are called "the mouths of the Amazon." Many islands lie between the channels.

Macapá and Belém are two large Brazilian cities at the mouths of the Amazon. Ships from Europe and the United States enter **ports** at the cities.

11

Chapter 3

Exploring the Amazon

In the 1500s, Europeans began to explore South America. Spanish explorer Vicente Yáñez Pinzón was probably the first European to see the Amazon. Pinzón's ship sailed on the Atlantic Ocean near the coast of South America. The sailors tasted some of the water. It was not salty. They wanted to know why. They sailed toward some land in the distance. Their ship soon reached the mouth of the Amazon.

Pinzón sailed about 60 miles (100 kilometers) up the wide river. The freshwater he and the sailors tasted in the ocean came from this river.

Exploring the Amazon was not easy. Thick forests made travel through the area difficult.

In 1541, Spaniard Francisco de Orellana was the first European to explore the Amazon. He led a group of men from the mouth of the Napo River to the Atlantic Ocean.

Stories of Orellana's trip made other Europeans want to come to South America. People from Spain and Portugal came to live in the Amazon River **basin**.

Exploring the Rain Forest

In the late 1700s, French and British explorers came to study the plants and trees in the rain forest. They saw a white, sticky sap coming from some trees. They learned the sap could be made into rubber.

F A C T !

Some people think the Amazon River was named after the Amazons. The Amazons were women warriors in ancient Greek stories. Orellana said he saw a group of women warriors on his trip down the river. He compared the women to the Amazons.

People used rubber in shoes and bicycle tires. Europeans sold rubber from the Amazon in Europe and the United States. The rubber trade made some cities on the Amazon rich. Iquitos in Peru and Manaus and Belém in Brazil grew because of their ports near the river.

By 1915, people found rubber in other parts of the world. People in the Amazon basin no longer made money selling rubber. They looked for new ways to make money. In the 1960s, **mining** gold brought in needed money.

People tapped trees near the Amazon for sap to make into rubber.
◀

Chapter 4

The Amazon's People

For thousands of years, **native** people have lived near the Amazon River. The people travel on the river. They also use the river for food. They eat fish they catch in the river. Farmers grow vegetables on land near the river. Hunters kill wild animals in the rain forest for food.

Three to 5 million Indians lived near the Amazon when European explorers arrived in the 1500s. Today, fewer than 1 million Indians live throughout the Amazon rain forest. Europeans brought diseases that killed many of the Amazon's native people.

People living along the Amazon use boats to travel from place to place.

The Amazon's People Today

Today, much of the Amazon basin remains unexplored. Thick forests of trees and vines make travel through the area difficult. Groups of native people still live in these areas. Some groups have little contact with the outside world. Other Amazon Indians live and work in cities.

▲ Some homes along the Amazon are built on stilts. When the river floods, the homes stay safe.

Descendants of early settlers live in the cities along the river. Many of these settlers came from Portugal and Spain. Some people are also descendants of African slaves. These people were forced by Europeans to leave their homeland and work for free. Today, people in cities work in businesses or factories. They also farm or fish along the Amazon.

People living in cities along the Amazon catch fish in the river to sell at markets.

Chapter 5

Using the Amazon

The Amazon River and rain forest are filled with important **natural resources**. Today, fish, minerals, and wood are taken from the Amazon basin. People sell and trade these goods. People living along the Amazon depend on river trade to survive.

River Ports

River ports, such as Iquitos, Peru, and Manaus, Brazil, are centers for trade. People can reach the ports only by water or air. Roads do not go to Iquitos. Supplies for buildings, cars, and other goods must be brought to the city on ships or in airplanes.

People wait at docks along the river at Iquitos, Peru. Boats bring people and goods up the Amazon to Iquitos.

Fishing

Fishing is important to people living along the river. People who fish in Brazil hunt for pirarucu. It is one of the largest freshwater fish in the world. Pirarucu can grow to be 15 feet (4.6 meters) long. Fishers feed their families for days with the meat of one fish. They also sell the fish at ports on the Amazon.

The pirarucu is a huge fish that lives in ▼ the Amazon.

▲ Lumber floats on the river before being picked up to ship to ports on the Amazon.

FACT!

By the 1980s, people in the Amazon made almost $3 billion each year by selling gold.

Mining and Logging

Mining is another **industry** along the river. People mine gold, silver, and other minerals from the Amazon and its tributaries.

Trees growing along the Amazon are also a source of income. People cut down trees for lumber to build homes, furniture, and musical instruments.

Chapter 6

The Amazon Today

Years of using the Amazon basin's natural resources have harmed the land and the river. Today, people try to bring attention to the Amazon's problems. They run tourist trips that also bring in needed money to the area.

Damaging the Amazon

Cutting down trees harms animals. Fish in the river eat seeds and fruit that fall from trees. With fewer trees along the Amazon, the fish starve. People then do not catch as many fish to sell and trade.

Pollution also harms the Amazon. Gold mines along the Amazon and its tributaries pollute the river. Mercury is a chemical that gets into the rivers from gold mining. Mercury harms fish and other animals.

Trees along the Amazon are cut down to clear land for farming.

Sewage enters the Amazon from cities. Sewage is dirty water from toilets and other drains. The dirty water makes people sick and harms animals living in the river.

Tourism

Today, boats bring visitors up the Amazon. They see the rain forest and its wildlife. Tourist boats also stop at villages.

Cruise ships take tourists up and down the ▼ Amazon River.

Tourism brings money to the people living along the Amazon. Local people want to protect the Amazon so visitors continue to visit the Amazon River area.

The Amazon River gives life to everything around it. In the future, people will work to use the Amazon basin's resources without harming the river and the land around it.

Fast Facts

Source: streams in the Andes Mountains

Outlet: Atlantic Ocean

Name: named for the Amazon warriors in the stories of ancient Greece

Major tributaries: Negro River, Madeira River, Tapajós River, Xingu River, Napo River

Explorers: Vicente Yáñez Pinzón, Francisco de Orellana

Major industries: fishing, lumber, mining, farming

Major cities: Manaus and Belém, Brazil; Iquitos, Peru

Hands On: A River of Rivers

Some people say the Amazon is a river of rivers. Thousands of smaller rivers flow into the Amazon. These rivers add water and sediment to the Amazon. Try this activity to see how tributaries make a larger river.

What You Need
a large pan filled with tightly packed dirt
book
stick
friend
2 glasses of water

What You Do
1. Place a book underneath one side of the pan filled with dirt. The book will tilt the pan so the water runs downhill.
2. Make one long line in the dirt with the stick.
3. Next, make smaller lines in the dirt on either side of the line you made in Step 2. The smaller lines should join the first line.
4. Now, you and your friend should stand on either side of the pan. At the same time, you and your friend should slowly pour water from the glasses into the smaller lines. What happens as the water runs downhill?

Glossary

basin (BAY-suhn)—an area of land around a river from which water drains into the river

channel (CHAN-uhl)—a narrow stretch of water between two areas of land

descendant (di-SEND-uhnt)—a person's children and family members born after those children

industry (IN-duh-stree)—businesses that make products or provide services

mine (MINE)—to remove gold, diamonds, copper, or other minerals from the ground

native (NAY-tiv)—belonging to an area

natural resource (NACH-ur-uhl REE-sorss)—a material found in nature that is useful to people

port (PORT)—a place where boats and ships can dock or anchor safely

sediment (SED-uh-muhnt)—bits of rock and sand mixed with mud and carried by water

tributary (TRIB-yoo-tar-ee)—a river that flows into another larger river

Internet Sites

FactHound offers a safe, fun way to find Internet sites related to this book. All of the sites on FactHound have been researched by our staff.

Here's how:
1. Visit *www.facthound.com*
2. Type in this special code **0736824820** for age-appropriate sites. Or enter a search word related to this book for a more general search.
3. Click on the **Fetch It** button.

FactHound will fetch the best sites for you!

Read More

Meister, Cari. *Amazon River.* Rivers and Lakes. Edina, Minn.: Abdo, 2002.

Parker, Edward. *The Amazon.* Great Rivers of the World. Milwaukee: World Almanac Library, 2003.

Index